Choose Your Future

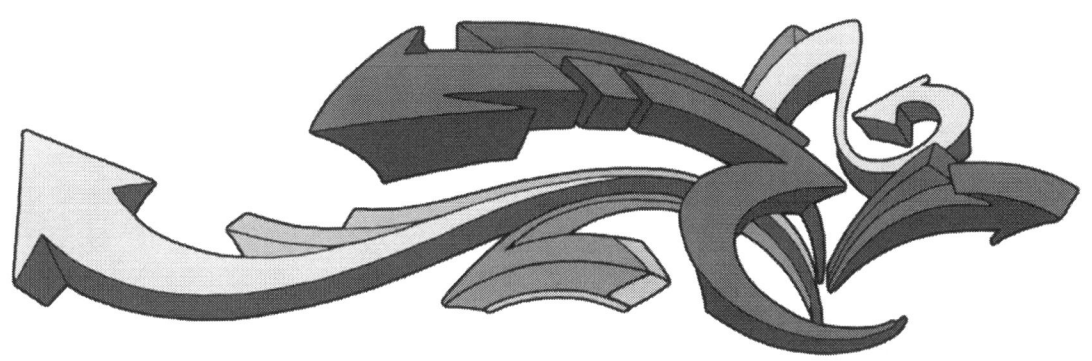

Exploring

Science   Technology   Engineering   Mathematics

Activity Book

Grades 5 - 9

Instructions

This book will help you get started deciding what types of work interest you.

- This is not another school homework assignment, it is **Sortafunwork.**

- Do these activities when It is **cold, hot, rainy, windy, you are bored, you want to get out of doing homework, housework, cleaning the bathroom or dog kennel.**

Instructions continued

- Take your time, even years is OK. It is a long time before you actually need to know this information. You might even want to read it after you graduate from high school or college.

- Pick and choose the activities that interest you. Do all, some, or even none, but at least read the activity book.

- Color, don't color, color however you want.

- **Save the book for future reference**. It is also fun to look back and see how your interests have changed.

Learning one thing that helps you make better decisions will save you and your parents many times the price of this activity book. **When you are about 30 years old, you will know if you did enough *Sortafunwork*.**

Incomes shown in the activities are the **median average for the U.S.** Median average means middle - 50% earn more and 50% earn less. Occasionally you will see ++ after the income because these occupations earn way more than the income shown. A person starting out in an occupation will earn much less and an experienced person will earn much more. When researching a career, look at the **beginning, average, and top**. Incomes also vary from state to state and city to city.

Biochemists & Biophysicists   Source – Bureau of Labor Statistics

Location	10%	25%	Median	75%	90%
United States	$42,700	$57,700	$84,300	$114,000	$147,600
Idaho	$31,300	$33,600	$37,300	$66,800	$94,400
California	$50,400	$66,300	$92,400	$122,000	$163,800

Operations Research Analysts

United States	$42,070	$56,110	$74,630	$99,210	$130,210
Rhode Island	$35,220	$42,880	$60,940	$92,470	$135,480
Texas	$45,640	$55,110	$73,160	$99,210	$113,810

The decisions you make today, will affect the rest of your life.

Career Fields, Clusters, Pathways, & Careers

Choosing a career will be one of the hardest, most important decisions you will make in your life. Due to the overwhelming number of career choices, it helps to organize your options. The following is one way to organize your search.

The **6 Career Fields** are the broadest level of career options. They are a good place to start exploring careers.

Underneath the six Career Fields are **16 Career Clusters**. The clusters include more details about the careers that interest you. Careers in each cluster have been grouped according to knowledge and skills that are needed in that cluster. Each cluster may include hundreds of careers.

Each career cluster includes one or more of **81 Career Pathways**. A pathway is made up of related career specialties within a career cluster.

Beneath the Pathways are **800+ Careers**.

Engineering, Manufacturing, & Technology Career Field

Science, Technology, Engineering, & Math Cluster

- ❑ Is science one of your favorite subjects?
- ❑ Do you prepare projects for science fairs?
- ❑ Do you enjoy reading science magazines?
- ❑ Are you detail-oriented?
- ❑ Do you want to know how things work?
- ❑ Do you like to visit museums?
- ❑ Do you like to take things apart and out them back together?
- ❑ Do you like to learn what makes the best explosions and eruptions?

If you answered yes to two or more of the above questions, you might be interested in considering a career in Science, Technology, Engineering, or Mathematics.

Science & Mathematics Pathway

Careers in these pathways apply knowledge and skills in the real world. Your goal would be to improve the physical & human environment. In your work, you would engage in discovery to gather and process data to solve problems. Check careers that interest you today.

Science & Mathematics Careers

- ❏ Anthropologists
- ❏ Archaeologists
- ❏ Astronomers
- ❏ Biologists
- ❏ Cartographers & Photogrammetrists
- ❏ Chemists
- ❏ Environmental Scientists
- ❏ Geographers
- ❏ Geologists & Geophysicists
- ❏ Historians
- ❏ Mathematicians
- ❏ Meteorologists
- ❏ Natural Science Managers
- ❏ Physicists
- ❏ Political Scientists
- ❏ Remote Sensing Scientists
- ❏ Remote Sensing Technologists
- ❏ Science Technicians
- ❏ Sociologists

Engineering & Technology Pathway

Careers in these pathways solve problems involving design, development, or production. You would work on projects to evaluate problems and develop and test solutions. You could also provide advice and consultation. Check careers that interest you today.

Engineering & Technology Careers

❑ Aerospace Engineers

❑ Architectural & Engineering Managers

❑ Civil Engineers

❑ Electrical & Electronics Engineers

❑ Electronics Engineering Technologists

❑ Energy Engineers

❑ Engineering Technicians

❑ Environmental Engineering Technicians

❑ Geographic Information Systems Specialists

❑ Geospatial Information Scientists & Technologists

❑ Industrial Engineers

❑ Manufacturing Engineering Technologists

❑ Manufacturing Engineers

❑ Materials Engineers

❑ Mechanical Engineers

❑ Mining Engineers

❑ Nuclear Engineers

❑ Petroleum Engineers

❑ Photonics Engineers

❑ Robotics Engineers

❑ Validation Engineers

❑ Wind Energy Engineers

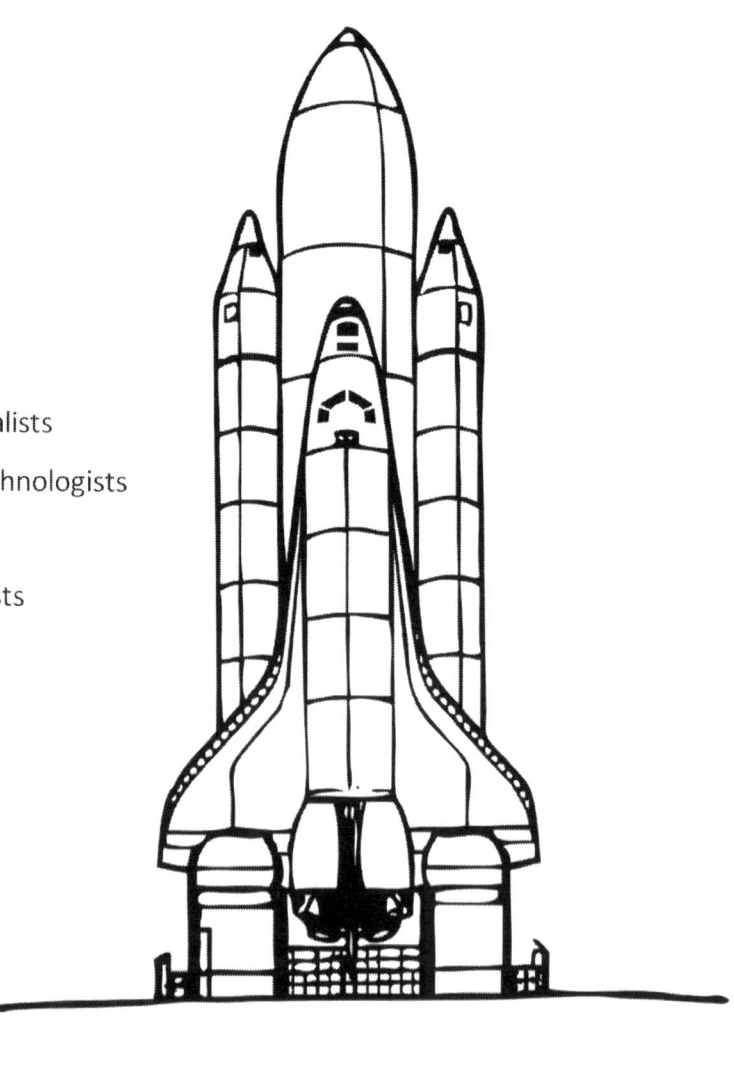

Types of Colleges & Universities

Check the type of school you would like to attend. Also check the type of degree you would like to earn.

- ❑ **Public Colleges** – Colleges that receive money from taxes.
- ❑ **In-State Colleges** – Tuition is less for students living in the state.
- ❑ **Out of State Colleges** – Tuition is usually higher for students who do not live in the state. Occasionally neighboring states will allow students to enroll and not pay out of state tuition.
- ❑ **Private Colleges** – Receive no tax help from the government. Tuition is usually higher than public schools.
- ❑ **For Profit Colleges** – Colleges that are run like a business. Tuitions are usually very high because they are trying to make a profit.
- ❑ **Junior Colleges / Community Schools** - Two year schools. Tuition is usually less than 4-year schools. Credits are often transferable to a 4-year school.

Types of Degrees

It is important to know how much training is required to work in an occupation that interests you. Additional education and training **do not guarantee success**. It will often provide you with tools to move forward in a career, open up jobs that interest you, and provide you greater security.

- ❑ **Certificates & Diplomas** - These programs are less than 2 yrs. and allow you to step right into a specific occupation.
- ❑ **Associate & Degrees** -   Most take 2 years to complete, and some can be used to obtain a bachelor's degree.
- ❑ **Bachelor's Degree** - These usually take 4 – 5 years to complete.
- ❑ **Master's Degree** - These programs take an additional 1 – 2 years after you complete your bachelor's.
- ❑ **Advanced Degrees** - These programs take an additional 3 years beyond bachelor's or master's degrees.

What are your after high school plans today? It is ok to change the plans later.

_____

_____

Bankers (Managers)

Keep our money safe. They like to lead and persuade customers to buy more of their banking products and services. $61,300/yr. $115,320/yr. $187,200/yr.   4 yrs. college   Very large occupation.   Faster than average growth.   Very high number of annual openings.   Level of interest 1 2 3 4 5

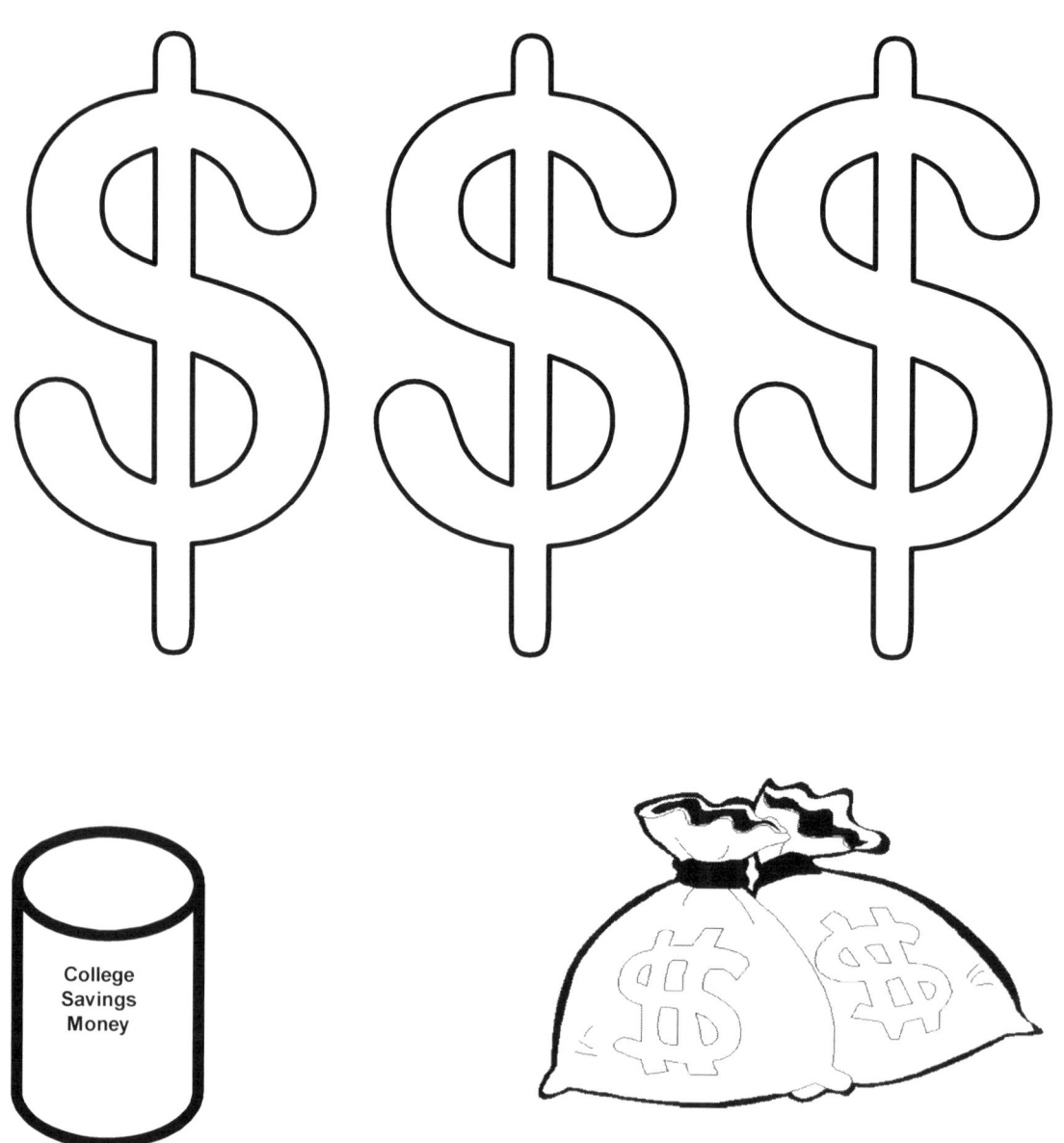

Animal Breeders

Select and breed animals and pets. $18,400/yr. $40,000/yr. $$63,200/yr. 1-2 yrs. college Very small occupation. Slower than average growth. Very few annual openings. Level of interest 1 2 3 4 5

Exploring STEM Occupations Activity Book

Firefighters

Put out fires and teach us about fire safety. Must like helping people, solving hands- on problems and working outside in all types of weather.

$22,000/yr. $45,940/yr. $80,400/yr.   1-4 yrs. college   Very large occupation.

Slower than average growth.   Very high number of annual openings.

Level of interest 1 2 3 4 5

Exploring STEM Occupations Activity Book

STEM Occupations & Tools

Match the tools used with the appropriate occupation. Indicate your level of interest. Pick the two occupations that interest you today and complete the chart.

onetonline.org   Occupation Quick Search   Tools & Technology

	Occupation		Tools
1 2 3 4 5	1. Aerospace Engineering Technician – Operate instruments used to launch spacecraft.	C	A. Automated soldering machines, electronic measuring probes, frequency analyzer, signal generator, voltage meter.
1 2 3 4 5	2. Atmospheric Scientist – Prepare weather reports & forecasts for the public.		B. Fishing net, aerial nets, sporting traps, map creation software.
1 2 3 4 5	3. Civil Drafter – Prepare drawings & maps used in civil engineering projects.		C. Calipers, punches or nail sets, taps, vibration testers, welder torch.
1 2 3 4 5	4. Electrical Engineer – Assist engineer test machinery in factories or laboratories.		D. Hard hat, safety glasses, plotter printer, CAD software.
1 2 3 4 5	5. Computer User Support Specialist – Provide technical assistance to computer users.		E. Moisture meters, automated land-leveling systems, sprayer application equipment.
1 2 3 4 5	6. Forest & Conservation Worker – Pull trees, plant trees, build erosion breaks.		F. Air pollution sampler, decibel meter, compliance software, CAD software.
1 2 3 4 5	7. Fuel Cell Technicians – Work with fuel cell systems.		G. Digital camera, physiological recorder, decibel meter, oxygen analyzer.
1 2 3 4 5	7. Graphic Designer – Design or create graphics for packaging, displays, logos, etc.		H. Curves, CAD programs, wide-format scanners, estimating keypads.
1 2 3 4 5	8. Human Factors Engineer (Ergonomics) – Design objects & facilities to optimize human well being & system performance.		I. Shovel, saw, ladder, brush hog, planting drill, backpack sprayer.
1 2 3 4 5	9. Industrial Safety Engineer – Plan & coordinate safety programs.	F	J. Force gauges, tension meters, thickness measuring devices, ultrasonic flaw detectors.
1 2 3 4 5	10. Marine Architect - Design ships, barges, submarines, tugs, etc.		K. Power meters, lab convection ovens, solar radiation surface observing tools.
1 2 3 4 5	11. Nursery & Greenhouse Manager – Supervise greenhouse & nursery workers.		L. Air temperature recorders, anemometers, hygrometers, rainfall recorders.
1 2 3 4 5	12. Precision Agricultural Technician – Apply GIS & GPS systems to agricultural production.		M. Flow meters, multi-meters, voltage meters, altitude test chambers, scientific calculator.
1 2 3 4 5	13. Quality Control Analyst – Conduct tests to study quality of raw materials or products.		N. Laser printers, graphics image software, computer, scanner.
1 2 3 4 5	14. Solar Energy Systems Engineer – Evaluate sites for solar energy projects.		O. Computer tool kits, backup software, patch software, remote control software.
1 2 3 4 5	15. Wildlife Biologist – Study the characteristics & habitats of wildlife.		P. Irrigation equipment, pruning shears, sprayers, spreadsheet software.

	Income	Education	Why occupation appeals to you today.

Exploring STEM Occupations Activity Book

Meteorologists

Study the earth's atmosphere and how it effects our environment. Must like to investigate and work outdoors. $49,300/yr. $87,000/yr. $129,800/yr. 4-6 yrs. college Medium size occupation. Average growth. Moderate number of annual openings. Level of interest 1 2 3 4 5

Veterinarians

Treat animal health problems.

Must like to investigate, figure out problems mentally, and deal with animals that are sick or injured.

$44,200/yr. $87,590/yr. $149,500/yr.   Large occupation.   Slower than average growth.

Large number of annual openings.   Level of interest 1 2 3 4 5

Why is it harder to become a veterinarian than it is to become a physician?

_____

Vet every rarity schools de mainta ad lschool ʃ

Exploring STEM Occupations Activity Book

"Play 'em all. I played every game possible."

Jake Plummer, Former NFL Quarterback
Idaho Statesman April 23, 2015

The variety of sports helped him. "It was really good for my body, you have to adapt to new sports and a whole new way of moving." Plummer encourages kids to play as many sports as they can. He encourages coaches and parents to make the sports their children play enjoyable. Make the experience one to remember. Encourage them to continue to play sports their whole life - play 'em all. He also remembers being excited if there was a pizza party more than if we won or lost.

Dentists

Help us have healthy teeth and gums. Must like people and are detail oriented. $72,200/yr. $149,540/yr. $187,200/yr.   9 yrs. college

Medium size occupation.   Average growth.   Moderate number of annual openings.

Level of interest 1 2 3 4 5

Exploring STEM Occupations Activity Book

Chemists

Test chemicals and do experiments in labs.   Need to be social and like to investigate. $41,800 /yr. $73,480/yr. $122,800/yr.   4+ yrs. college   Small occupation.   Slower than average growth.   Few annual openings.

Level of interest 1 2 3 4 5

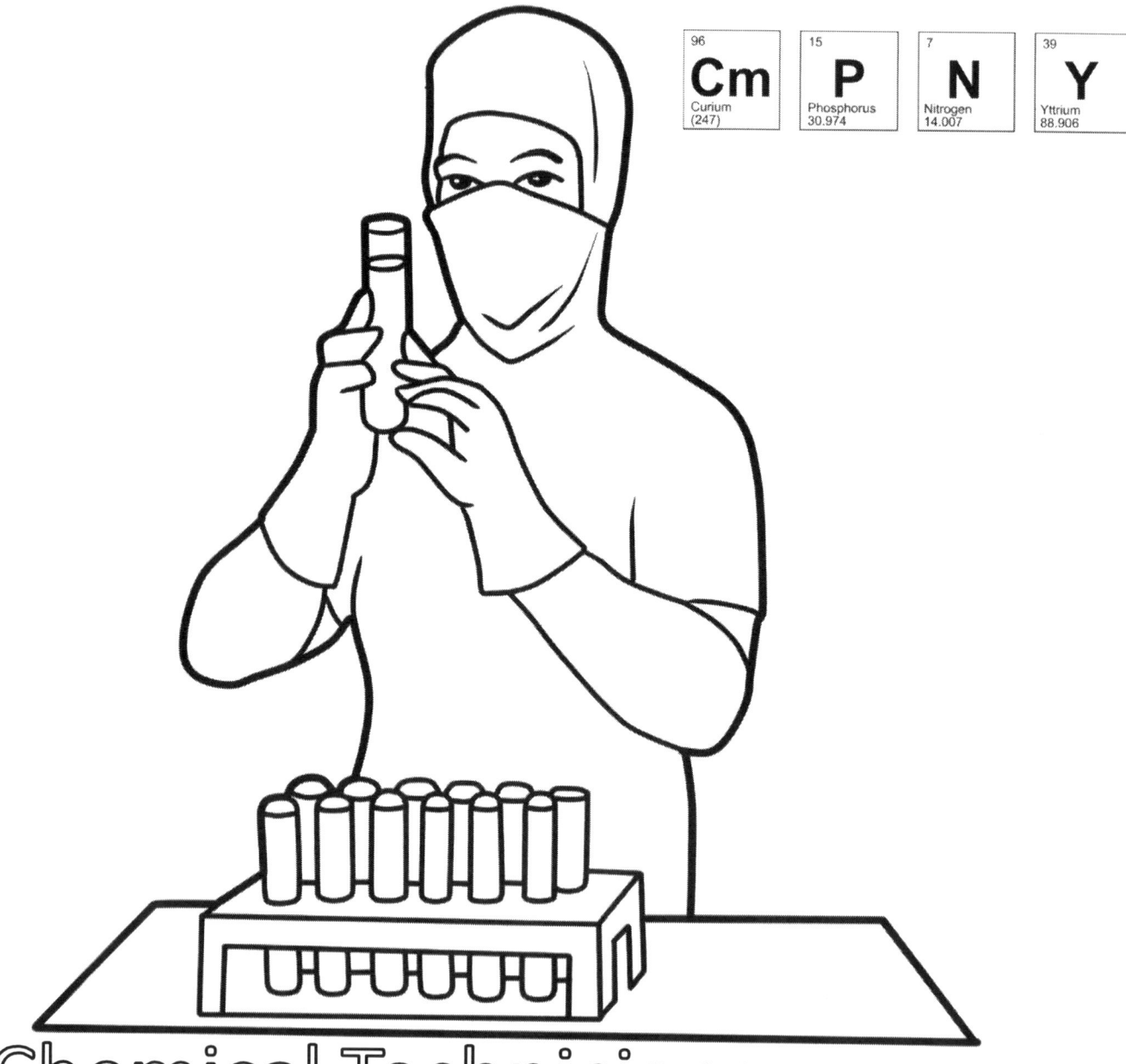

Chemical Technicians

Help chemists. $26,500/yr. $44,180/yr. $75,000/yr.   2+ yrs. college   Small occupation.   Slower than average growth.   Few annual openings.   Level of interest 1 2 3 4 5

Exploring STEM Occupations Activity Book

Accountants

Advise clients about their financial and tax needs. Must be able to explain this information in ways the client understands. $40,370/yr. $65,080/yr. $113,370/yr.   4 yrs. college   Very large occupation.   Average growth.   Very high number on annual openings.

Level of interest 1 2 3 4 5

Architects

Plan and design all types of buildings and structures. Draw or use a computer to create the plans. $44,900/yr. $74,500/yr. $121,900/yr.   4 yrs. college   Small occupation.   Average growth.   Few annual openings.   Level of interest 1 2 3 4 5

Exploring STEM Occupations Activity Book

Realtors

Sell residential property, commercial property, and apartments. Appraise the value of properties and suggest ways to increase value.   HS + $21,500/yr. $41,000/yr. $105,300/yr.   Large occupation.   Faster than average growth.   High number of annual openings.   Level of interest 1 2 3 4 5

Exploring STEM Occupations Activity Book

Civil Engineers

Supervise large construction projects. Must know the tools and methods to construct the project.   4 yrs. college $51,810/yr. $80,770/yr. $126,190/yr.   Large occupation. Average growth.   High number of annual openings.   Level of interest 1 2 3 4 5

Exploring STEM Occupations Activity Book

Construction Managers

Schedule and coordinate work on construction projects. Must be able to maintain the schedule and the budget. $50,200/yr. $85,630/yr. $146,300/yr.   4 yrs. college   Very large occupation.   Average growth.   Very high number of annual openings.

Exploring STEM Occupations Activity Book

Construction Related Occupations

Indicate occupations that interest you.

- ❏ Architect
- ❏ Landscape Architect
- ❏ Architectural & Civil Drafter
- ❏ Architectural & Engineering Manager
- ❏ Civil Engineering Technician
- ❏ Civil Engineer
- ❏ Drafter
- ❏ Electrical Engineer
- ❏ Electrical Drafter
- ❏ Electrical Engineering Technician
- ❏ Electro-Mechanical Technician
- ❏ Electro-Mechanical Technologist
- ❏ Engineering Technician
- ❏ Electrical Engineering Technologist
- ❏ Engineering Teacher
- ❏ Mechanical Drafter
- ❏ Mechanical Engineering Technician
- ❏ Mechanical Engineering Technologist
- ❏ Mechanical Engineer
- ❏ Nuclear Engineer
- ❏ Nuclear Engineering Technician
- ❏ Surveying & Mapping Technician
- ❏ Surveyor
- ❏ Survey Researcher
- ❏ Drone Operator
- ❏ Boilermaker
- ❏ Carpenter
- ❏ Construction & Building Inspector
- ❏ Cost Estimator
- ❏ Electrician
- ❏ Elevator Installers
- ❏ Plumber, Pipefitter, & Steam Fitter
- ❏ Sheet Metal Worker
- ❏ Structural Iron & Steel Worker
- ❏ Tile & Marble Setter
- ❏ Urban & Regional Planners
- ❏ Wind Turbine Designer
- ❏ Wind Turbine Installer

Make a list of additional construction company occupations.

- ❏ Accountant
- ❏ Administrative Assistant
- ❏ _____
- ❏ _____
- ❏ _____
- ❏ _____
- ❏ _____
- ❏ _____
- ❏ _____
- ❏ _____
- ❏ _____
- ❏ _____
- ❏ _____
- ❏ _____
- ❏ _____
- ❏ _____

Line Persons

Install or repair electrical wire distribution systems. May also erect poles and transmission towers. Must like working outdoors in all types of weather.   High School+ $35,100/yr. $65,900/yr. $94,000/yr.   Large occupation.   Faster than average growth.   High number of annual openings.

Level of interest 1 2 3 4 5

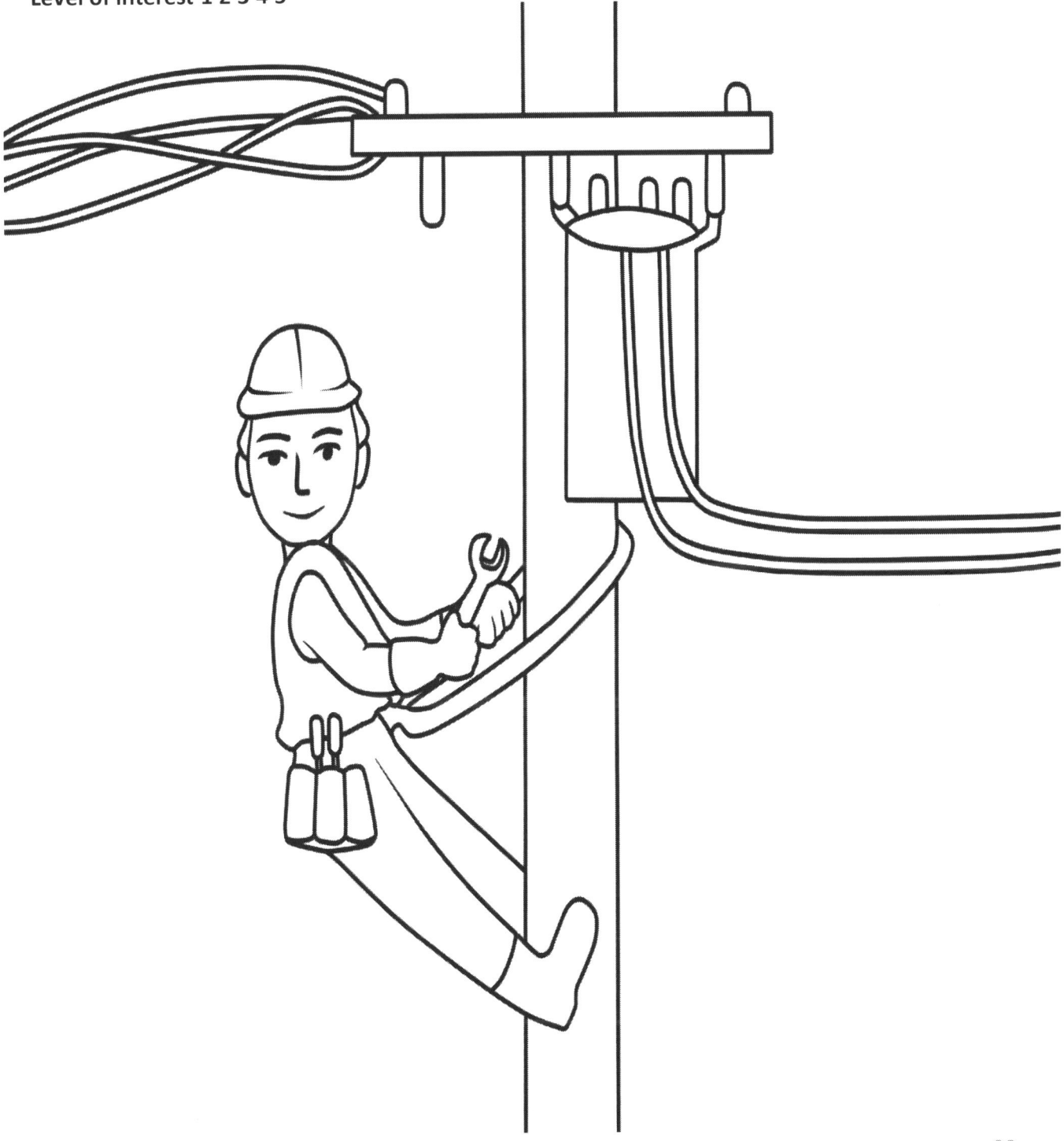

Astronauts

Operate and work aboard spacecraft and the space station. Helpful, but not required to have flying experience. $141,117/yr. 4 yrs.+ college Extremely small occupation. Very little growth. Very few annual openings.

Level of interest 1 2 3 4 5

Exploring STEM Occupations Activity Book

STEM Occupation Research

Go the website of a computer technology company that would hire STEM occupations. Look at employment opportunities to find positions that interest you. Read the job description to learn details of the position. Salary information can be found at onetonline.org Information is provided by the U.S. Dept. of Labor and the website is safe and free. Rate level of interest 1 2 3 4 5. Example: Micron Technology has a very large list of positions that you have never heard of that are located all over the world.

Position & Brief Job Description	Education Requirements	Salary	Level of Interest
			1 2 3 4 5
			1 2 3 4 5
			1 2 3 4 5
			1 2 3 4 5
			1 2 3 4 5
			1 2 3 4 5
			1 2 3 4 5
			1 2 3 4 5
			1 2 3 4 5

Exploring STEM Occupations Activity Book

STEM Occupation Research

Using onetonline.org. go to STEM Occupations to complete the following chart. Now is the time to look at lots of occupations. You have plenty of time to narrow down your choices as you get older. **Always have a Plan B**. One occupation using your head when the economy is good and another using your hands when the economy is not good.

Occupation	Trends U.S. & Local	Industries That Hire	Companies That Hire	Level of Interest 1 2 3 4 5
				1 2 3 4 5
				1 2 3 4 5
				1 2 3 4 5
				1 2 3 4 5
				1 2 3 4 5
				1 2 3 4 5
				1 2 3 4 5
				1 2 3 4 5
				1 2 3 4 5
				1 2 3 4 5
				1 2 3 4 5
				1 2 3 4 5
				1 2 3 4 5
				1 2 3 4 5

Astronomers

Study the sun, moon, stars, planets, and galaxies. They like to search for facts and figure out solutions to problems of the universe. $51,700/yr. $105,410/yr. $170,200/yr. This occupation is so small; no additional information is available. Level of interest 1 2 3 4 5

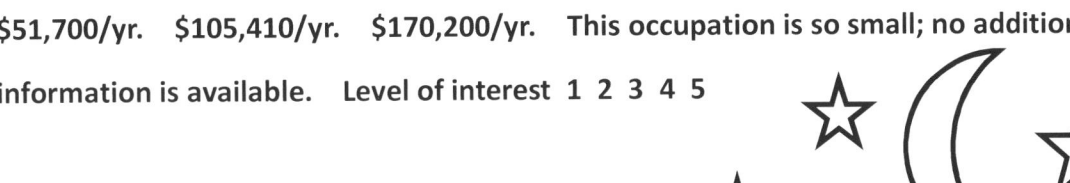

Aerospace Engineers

Design, test, and construct parts for aircraft, spacecraft, and weapons. They like to work in jobs where they get recognized for their work and are able to instruct others. $48,700/yr. $106,380/yr. $150,700/yr.   4+ yrs. college   Additional info. N.A.   Level of interest 1 2 3 4 5

Similar positions include:

- Pilots
- Bioengineers
- Level of interest 1 2 3 4 5

Safety Engineers

Look for ways to prevent accidents. Consider good working conditions important. $45,700/yr. $81,830/yr. $120,800/yr. 4+ yrs. college   Small occupation.   Faster than average growth.   Few annual openings.

Level of interest 1 2 3 4 5

Similar positions include:

- Mining Engineers
- Construction Managers
- Fire Investigators.

Level of interest 1 2 3 4 5

**Accident Free
174
Days**

Occupational Health & Safety Specialists

Recommend ways to improve health hazards. Usually like jobs where they are looked up to by others. $40,500/yr. $69,210/yr. $98,500/yr. 4+ yrs. college   Small occupation. Faster than average growth.   Moderate number of annual openings.   Level of interest 1 2 3 4 5

Similar positions include:

- Compliance Inspectors
- Building Inspectors
- Emergency Management Specialists
- Forensic Science Technicians

Level of interest 1 2 3 4 5

Accidents

Last Year 24   This Year 17

Nuclear Engineers
Design and operate nuclear facilities, including power plants. Prefer jobs where they are trained well.

$67,000/yr. $100,410/yr. $157,000/yr.   4-6 yrs. college   Small occupation.

Faster than average growth.   Moderate number of annual openings.

Level of interest 1 2 3 4 5

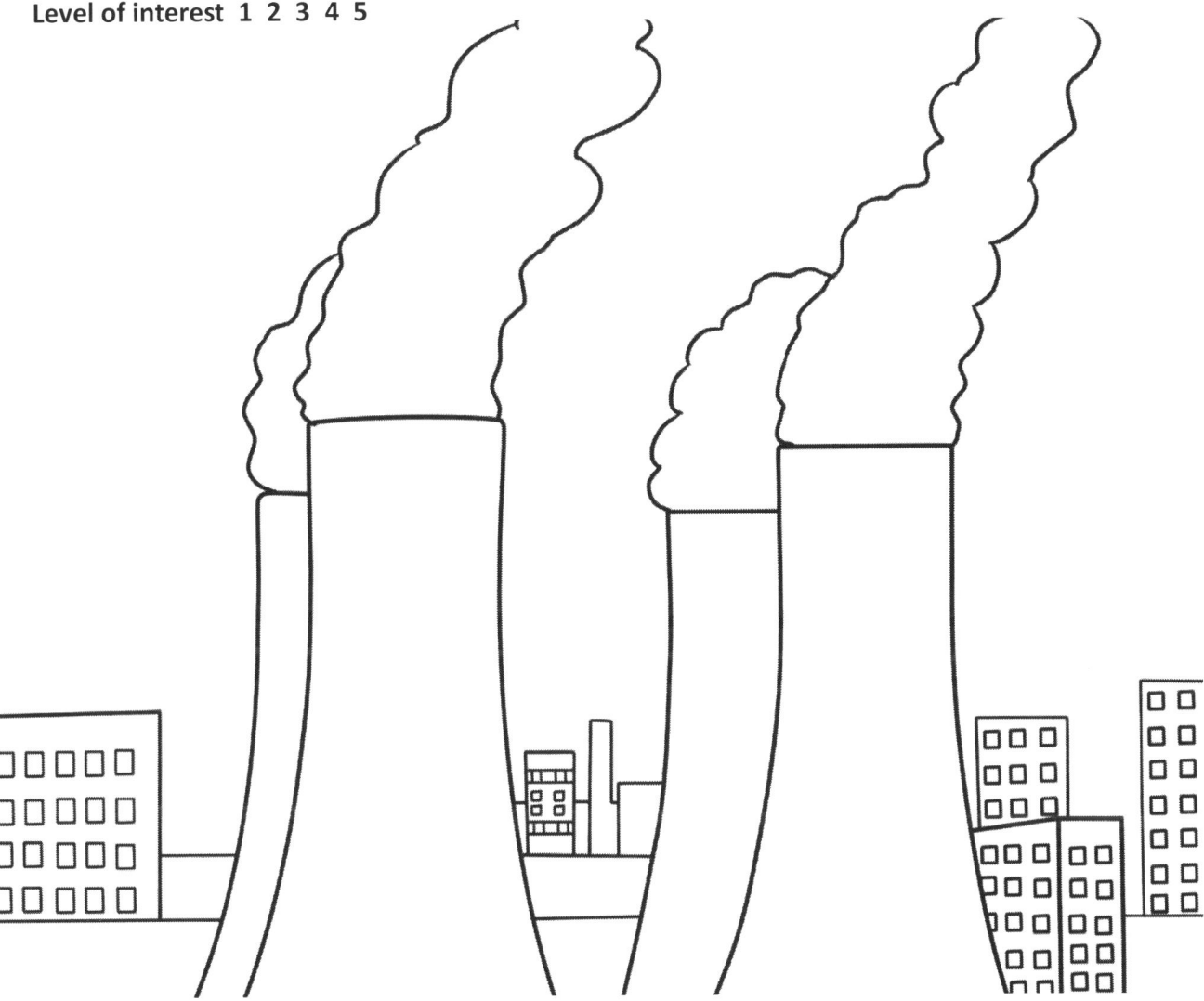

Nuclear Technicians
Help Nuclear Scientists conduct tests and experiments. Consider support from their employer important.

$46,300/yr. $74,690/yr. $96,200/yr.   1-4 yrs. college   Very large occupation.

Average growth.   Very high number of annual openings.   Level of interest 1 2 3 4 5

Exploring STEM Occupations Activity Book

Engineering Branches
Indicate areas of interest.

- ❏ Chemical Engineering
  - ❏ Biomolecular Engineering
  - ❏ Materials Engineering
  - ❏ Process Engineering

- ❏ Civil Engineering
  - ❏ Environmental Engineering
  - ❏ Geotechnical Engineering
  - ❏ Structural Engineering
  - ❏ Transport Engineering
  - ❏ Water Resources Engineering

- ❏ Electrical Engineering
  - ❏ Computer Engineering
  - ❏ Electronic Engineering
  - ❏ Optical Engineering
  - ❏ Power Engineering

- ❏ Mechanical Engineering
  - ❏ Acoustical Engineering
  - ❏ Manufacturing Engineering
  - ❏ Thermal Engineering
  - ❏ Vehicle Engineering

- ❏ Systems Engineering

- ❏ Interdisciplinary
  - ❏ Aerospace Engineering
  - ❏ Agricultural Engineering
  - ❏ Applied Engineering
  - ❏ Biological Engineering
  - ❏ Building Services Engineering
  - ❏ Energy Engineering
  - ❏ Railway Engineering
  - ❏ Industrial Engineering
  - ❏ Mechatronics Engineering
  - ❏ Military Engineering
  - ❏ Nanoengineering
  - ❏ Nuclear Engineering
  - ❏ Petroleum Engineering

Engineering Specialties
The following is a partial list of specialties.

- ❏ Metallurigical Engineering
- ❏ Ceramic Engineering
- ❏ Polymer Engineering
- ❏ Crystal Engineering
- ❏ Petroleum Refinery Engineering
- ❏ Plastics Engineering
- ❏ Paper Engineering
- ❏ Textile Engineering
- ❏ Ecological Engineering
- ❏ Fire Protection Engineering
- ❏ Sanitary Engineering
- ❏ Municipal or Urban Engineering
- ❏ Mining Engineering
- ❏ Foundation Engineering
- ❏ Earthquake Engineering
- ❏ Wind Engineering
- ❏ Architectural Engineering
- ❏ Ocean Engineering
- ❏ Traffic Engineering
- ❏ Highway Engineering
- ❏ Railway Systems Engineering
- ❏ Hydraulic Engineering
- ❏ River Engineering
- ❏ Coastal Engineering
- ❏ Groundwater Engineering
- ❏ Software Engineering
- ❏ Hardware Engineering
- ❏ Network Engineering
- ❏ Control Engineering
- ❏ Telecommunications Engineering
- ❏ Automotive Engineering
- ❏ Naval Engineering
- ❏ Aerospace Engineering
- ❏ Aeronautics
- ❏ Astronautics
- ❏ Aquaculture Engineering
- ❏ Biological Engineering
- ❏ Biomechanical Engineering
- ❏ Bioprocess Engineering
- ❏ Biotechnical Engineering
- ❏ Ecological Engineering

Machinists

Make parts out of metal and plastic that are found in nearly everything that is produced. They need computer and math skills. Close is never good enough, must be precise. $24,300/yr. $39,980/yr. $60,100/yr.   HS+ OJT, 1-2 yrs. college   Large occupation.   Faster than average growth.   High number of annual openings.

Level of interest 1 2 3 4 5

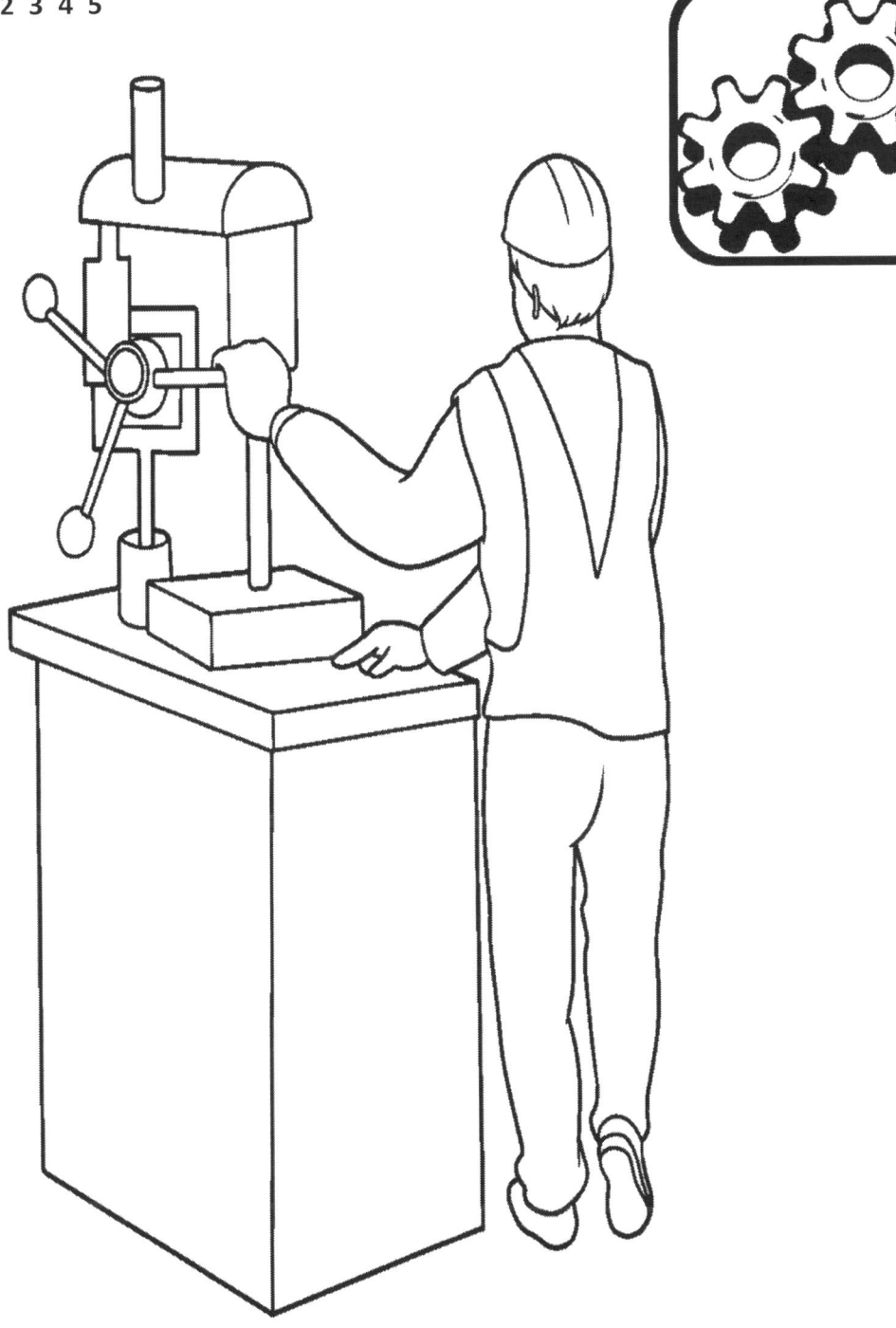

Exploring STEM Occupations Activity Book

STEM Occupations & Your Vocational Interests

Below is a sample list of STEM Careers. Rate each career using the **People, Data (information), or Things (tools) Criteria.** Most careers are a combination of two criteria. Example: Teaching – People & Data (P & D). Some might include all three.
Best Guesses are acceptable.

P & D	Cost Estimator		Video Game Designer
	Pharmacy Technicians		Nanosystems Engineers
	Computer Science Teacher		Optometrist
	Park Rangers		Computer Support Specialist
	Auto Master Mechanics		Registered Nurse
	Retardant Pilots (Wildfires)		Information Security Analyst
	Computer Operator		Surgeons
	Orthodontist		Faller
	Forensic Science Technician		Veterinary Assistant
	Surveyor		Animal Breeder
	Pediatrician		Nuclear Medical Technologist
	College Engineering Professor		Nursery & Greenhouse Managers
	Landscape Architect		Transportation Inspector
	Conservation Technician		Electrical Engineer
	Food Inspector		Occupational Therapist
	Veterinarian		Construction Manager
	Civil Engineer		Accountant
	Physical Therapist		Machinist
	Welder		Medical Sonographer
	Cook		Roadie - Broadcast Technician
	Climate Change Analyst		Fish & Game Warden
	Dental Hygienist		Bookkeeper
	Agricultural Technician		Fuel Cell Technician
	Fixed Wing Aircraft Mechanic		Farm & Ranch Manager

Exploring STEM Occupations Activity Book

Industrial Machinery Repairers

Maintain and repair factory equipment and machinery. They like practical, hands-on problem solving, and taking things apart and putting them back together. $31,000/yr. $46,630/yr. $71,900/yr. High School + On-the-Job Training Small occupation. Slower than average growth. Few annual openings.

Level of interest 1 2 3 4 5

Industrial Electronics Repairers

Install, maintain and repair electronic equipment. Must be precise as mistakes can cause injuries. $33,100/yr. $54,640/yr. $75,200/yr. 1-2 yrs. college Small occupation. Slower than average growth. Few annual openings.

Level of interest 1 2 3 4 5

Computerized Machine Operators

Set up & maintain computerized machine tools. Must be precise as mistakes cause delays and cost the company money.

$23,700/yr. $36,440/yr. $54,100/yr. High School + On-the-Job Training Small occupation. Average growth. Few annual openings Level of interest 1 2 3 4 5

Tool & Die Makers

Produce tools, dies, and other special devices for machines to make products. Items may require precision drilling with one ten-thousands of an inch tolerance. $31,700/yr. $48,890/yr. $70,800/yr. HS+ OJT Very small occupation. Average growth. Very few annual openings.

Level of interest 1 2 3 4 5

Medical Injury Attorneys

Specialize in cases that involve injuries, medical malpractice, food poisoning, etc. They like to compete with their heads. $55,200/yr. $114,300/yr. $187,200++/yr. 9 yrs. college   Additional info. NA   Level of interest 1 2 3 4 5

Exploring STEM Occupations Activity Book

Attorney Specialties

Indicate specialties that interest you.

- ❏ Accident, Personal Injury, Property Damage
- ❏ Administrative & Government
- ❏ Adoption
- ❏ Agricultural – Livestock
- ❏ Appeals
- ❏ Arbitration or Mediation
- ❏ Aviation
- ❏ Banking
- ❏ Bankruptcy
- ❏ Business, Corporation & Partnership
- ❏ Civil Rights
- ❏ Collections
- ❏ Construction
- ❏ Consumer Rights
- ❏ Contracts
- ❏ Criminal
- ❏ Divorce & Family
- ❏ Driving (DUI/DWI)
- ❏ Elder Law
- ❏ Employment – Labor
- ❏ Environmental
- ❏ General Practice
- ❏ Immigration & Naturalization
- ❏ Insurance
- ❏ Juvenile
- ❏ Land Use & Zoning
- ❏ Landlord & Tenant
- ❏ Malpractice – Professional
- ❏ Medical
- ❏ Military
- ❏ Patent, Trademark & Copyright
- ❏ Real Estate
- ❏ Securities
- ❏ Sexual Harassment
- ❏ Social Security
- ❏ Taxes
- ❏ Transportation
- ❏ Trials
- ❏ Water
- ❏ Wills, Estate Planning, & Probate
- ❏ Workers' Compensation

Write a story about a case you would like to defend or prosecute.

Colleges & Universities

Draw doodles & mascots for your favorite colleges or junior colleges.

Name of School **Mascot**

Army Careers That Require STEM Classes

Indicate occupations that interest you.

Science

- ❏ Medical Laboratory Specialist
- ❏ Optical Laboratory Specialist
- ❏ Petroleum Laboratory Specialist
- ❏ Clinical Laboratory Specialist

Technology

- ❏ Computer Detection Systems Repairer
- ❏ Cryptologic Network Warfare Specialist
- ❏ Geospatial Intelligence Imagery Analyst
- ❏ Information Technology Specialist
- ❏ Microwave Systems Operator - Maintainer
- ❏ Military Intelligence
- ❏ Multichannel Transmission Systems Repairer
- ❏ Multimedia Illustrator
- ❏ Network Systems Switching Operator - Maintainer
- ❏ Radio & Communication Security
- ❏ Radio Operator - Maintainer
- ❏ Satellite Communication Systems Operator - Maintainer
- ❏ Signal Support Systems Specialist
- ❏ Test Measurement & Diagnostic Equipment Maintenance Specialist
- ❏ Air Defense Battle Management System Operator
- ❏ Field Artillery Tactical Data System Operator
- ❏ Special Forces Communication Sergeant
- ❏ Combat Documentation / Production Specialist
- ❏ Integrated Family of Test Equipment Operator - Maintainer
- ❏ Watercraft Operator
- ❏ Patriot Fire Control Enhanced Operator - Maintainer
- ❏ Patriot Launching System Enhanced Operator - Maintainer
- ❏ Cable Systems Installer
- ❏ Signals Collection Analyst

Engineering

- ❏ Combat Engineer
- ❏ Special Forces Engineer Sergeant
- ❏ Geospatial Engineer
- ❏ Horizontal Construction Engineer
- ❏ Technical Engineer
- ❏ Watercraft Engineer

Math

- ❏ Financial Management Specialist
- ❏ Ammunition Stock Control
- ❏ Geospatial Engineer
- ❏ Human Intelligence Inspector
- ❏ Automated Logistical Specialist
- ❏ Unit Supply Specialist

Rank the STEM areas according to your interest level.

1. _____
2. _____
3. _____
4. _____

Exploring STEM Occupations Activity Book

Careers Are Everywhere

Including the traffic jam you are sitting in.

List all of the different careers you can think of that are a result of this traffic jam. Next to each occupation listed, indicate + STEM occupation or x non-Stem occupation. It is ok to get help from driver.

Sitting in traffic jam.	Traveling through construction "War Zone."	Office jobs at the road construction office.	Offices of the government agencies associated with this traffic jam.	Jobs associated with the suppliers of products for this traffic jam.
Traffic Cop	Laborer	Receptionist	Accountant	Machinist

Draw a picture of one of the occupations associated with this traffic jam.

Exploring STEM Occupations Activity Book

Fish & Game Wardens

Enforce fish and game regulations. Investigate damage to property done by wildlife. $32,700/yr. $50,880/yr. $75,500/yr.   4+ yrs. college   Small occupation. Little or no growth. Few annual openings.   Level of interest 1 2 3 4 5

Forest Rangers

Protect our forests and help prevent wildfires. They like to work outdoors with plants, animals, tools, and machinery.

$37.200/yr. $57,980/yr. $83,400/yr.   4 yrs. college   Small occupation.

Average growth.   Few annual openings.   Level of interest 1 2 3 4 5

Exploring STEM Occupations Activity Book

Wildland Firefighters

Control and put out wildfires. They like to work outdoors, physical fitness is very important. $22,100/yr. $46,000/yr. $81,400/yr.   High School + 1   Small occupation.   Slower than average growth.   Few job openings.   Level of interest 1 2 3 4 5

Wildland Firefighter
Interest Inventory

Read activities & decide if you like it, are unsure, or don't like it today.	+	?	x
Work outdoors when it is hot, cold, raining, snowing, windy, & dusty.			
Sleep on the ground or in a tent for many days in a row.			
Eat freeze dried food, rations, MRIs, or catered meals.			
Travel in airplanes, helicopters, school busses, crew cabs, or trucks.			
Parachute, rappel, or hike to fires.			
Not be able to use your cell phone for several days.			
Work up to 16 hrs. for 13 days in a row, with only 1 day off.			
Not take a shower for several days.			
Being on call 24 hrs. a day, seven days a week for entire season.			
Only able to go home for emergencies or if you are injured while on fires.			
Never know how much money you are going to make each season.			
Be away from your spouse & kids for extended periods of time.			
Mostly very appreciated on fires but sometimes not appreciated.			
See forests, rangeland, desert, swamps, and tundra.			
Swat mosquitoes, horseflies, no see-ums & other biting insects.			
Dig hand line with a pulaski, shovel, rake, chainsaw, etc.			
Crawl around on the ground feeling out hot spots with your hands.			
Hurry up & wait. Hurry up & wait. Hurry up & wait. Hurry up & wait.			
Watch out for falling trees, rolling rocks, and lightning.			
Total your answers and decide if you want to be a wildland firefighter. Write short paragraph describing your feelings.			

_____

_____

_____

STEM Occupations

Find the words in the grid. Words can go across and down only.

```
C P M N R M N W A T E R R E S O U R C E S P E C I A L I S T
R N H K L R R K T W L L J L Y T N K R P B M P A C T U A R Y
Y L R M X K L M W M L V L C X C Y N K I B L Y G Y W T M K T
T R N G E N E T I C I S T M D V C X G D J K L T R W H K H P
S W R L R R L L Q X L H M Z W M A T H E M A T I C I A N L L
O L M V Y K D T Y R P Y T Z T Q N R W M F T D R L J N R N R
F X H Y Z R L V M N Q D M K R R N F Z I M D N B R J K X D N
T H Q Z X F M N H R P R M C R K X T C O T T K H Q M H R B E
W T F Z N N K L Q M C O D O L X V R P L N W R J T W R C K U
A M F T Y Z R R F K D L M O V L Y D N O C W M K J T Y G T R
R L G N Z N N K K J Z O M K P L N T N G T V R X F W R W X O
E K D I E T I T I A N G F V T N K J R I L Y W Z K R T P Y P
D R J Y C R G Y G M B I A K D C F D H S M M D T R K N W Z S
E L M L F N T J M Z H S R W D X P T L T V L J J R D H P X Y
V L R K Z Z H J F C H T M K P B F T L J X J R M B F L N Z C
E L T T N R Y T T F N L M V R M R Y Y F K G P L D N G F Z H
L T D V N N L L R T P T A J R D H P P R T T Z T T R M V K O
O B P E T R O L E U M E N G I N E E R F M W N T M P T Y K L
P N M G Z L K L B N L M A L L T N C G W D C K T N N Y R M O
E F W T T M D F B M G N G X R P L T L Y K L M Y R R M F L G
R N P N H T Z J M M Q R E J F O O D B A T C H M A K E R K I
K Z X D T V Q K G F B L R R R F K G R D M T L F F L L L S
H G N P N R C N R R M P M R C W L T Y L Y B Y W T M L G J T
```

Occupation	Duties & Responsibilities	Median Income	Education	1 2 3 4 5
Actuary	Analyze statistical data.	$96,700/yr.	4 yrs. college	1 2 3 4 5
Cook	Cook food for schools, hospitals, & cafeterias.	$23,440/yr.	High School	1 2 3 4 5
Dietitian	Plan food service or nutritional food programs.	$56,950/yr.	4-9 yrs. college	1 2 3 4 5
Epidemiologist	Investigate causes & distribution of diseases.	$67,420/yr.	6+ yrs. college	1 2 3 4 5
Food Batcher	Operate food manufacturing equipment.	$26,770/yr.	High School	1 2 3 4 5
Farm Manager	Manage farms & ranches.	$68,050/yr.	Info. NA	1 2 3 4 5
Geneticist	Study inheritance traits.	$74,720/yr.	9+ yrs. college	1 2 3 4 5
Mathematician	Solve problems using mathematical methods.	$103,720/yr.	6-9 yrs. college	1 2 3 4 5
Neuropsychologist	Diagnose & treat mental problems.	$92,110/yr.	9 yrs. college	1 2 3 4 5
Petroleum Engineer	Devise methods to improve oil & gas mining.	$130,050/yr.	4+yrs. college	1 2 3 4 5
Software Developer	Design software for operating systems.	$102,880/yr.	4 yrs. college	1 2 3 4 5
Water Resource Specialist	Solve water supply, quality, & compliance problems.	$130,050/yr.	4+ yrs. college	1 2 3 4 5

Exploring STEM Occupations Activity Book

Loggers

Build and repair roads, clear brush, cut & buck trees, move logs to mills and shipyards. Work outdoors in all kinds of weather. Wide variety of incomes. High School Large occupation. Declining growth. Very few annual openings. Level of interest 1 2 3 4 5

One of my many pay for college jobs was working on logging roads piling brush. I even worked with the powder monkey and got to set off some charges, which was way more exciting than piling brush.

Fallers

Cut down trees with chainsaws. One of the types of trees is called a "widow maker". High School $34,490/yr. Large occupation. Declining growth. Very few annual openings. Level of interest 1 2 3 4 5

Log Graders & Scalers

Estimate how much a log is worth. High School $35,430/yr. Small occupation. Declining growth. Few annual openings. Level of interest 1 2 3 4 5

Make a list of occupations required to get a log from the forest to a construction site. Check occupations that interest you and write a sentence explaining why the others do not interest you.

- ❏ 1. _____
- ❏ 2. _____
- ❏ 3. _____
- ❏ 4. _____
- ❏ 5. _____
- ❏ 6. _____
- ❏ 7. _____
- ❏ 8. _____

Mechanics, Installers, Repairers

Type of Mechanic/Installer	Education	Low	Median	High	Interest
Aircraft	High School + 1	$34,900	$57,000	$86,900	1 2 3 4 5
Bus, Truck, & Diesel Engines	High School + 1	$28,100	$43,600	$65,000	1 2 3 4 5
Auto (Master)	High School + 1	$20,800	$37,100	$62,300	1 2 3 4 5
Heavy Equipment	High School + 1	$31,800	$47,600	$69,000	1 2 3 4 5
Motorboat	High School + 1	$22,300	$37,300	$57,800	1 2 3 4 5
Refrigeration	High School + 1	$24,000	$44,600	$70,800	1 2 3 4 5
Farm Equipment	High School + 1	$23,000	$36,200	$53,800	1 2 3 4 5
Outdoor/Small Engine	High School + 1	$20,500	$32,100	$49,200	1 2 3 4 5
Industrial Machinery	High School + 1	$28,000	$48,000	$75,100	1 2 3 4 5
Motorcycle	High School + 1	$21,300	$34,000	454,100	1 2 3 4 5
Heating & Air Conditioning	High School + 1	$27,600	$44,600	$70,800	1 2 3 4 5
Radio	High School + 1	$27,900	$48,000	$75,100	1 2 3 4 5
Mechanic Supervisor	High School + 1	$37,400	$62,300	$96,300	1 2 3 4 5
Bicycle	High School	$20,900	$32,100	$49.200	1 2 3 4 5
Security & Fire Alarms	High School + 1	$26,700	$42,600	$63,400	1 2 3 4 5

Choose two of the occupations that interest you the most and complete the chart.
Use o*net online to complete the chart.

Occupation	Number Employed	% Change	Projected Job Openings

Exploring STEM Occupations Activity Book

Pilots

Fly injured or sick patients to a hospital. Must be able to work as part of a team of emergency care personnel. College preferred also military experience. Income information N.A. Small occupation. Average growth. Average number of annual openings.

Botanists

Research yield of agricultural plants and crops. Present results to interested groups of people. $35,900/yr. $59,900/yr. $100,900/yr.
6+ yrs. college   Medium size occupation.   Slower than average growth.
Moderate number of annual openings.   Level of interest 1 2 3 4 5

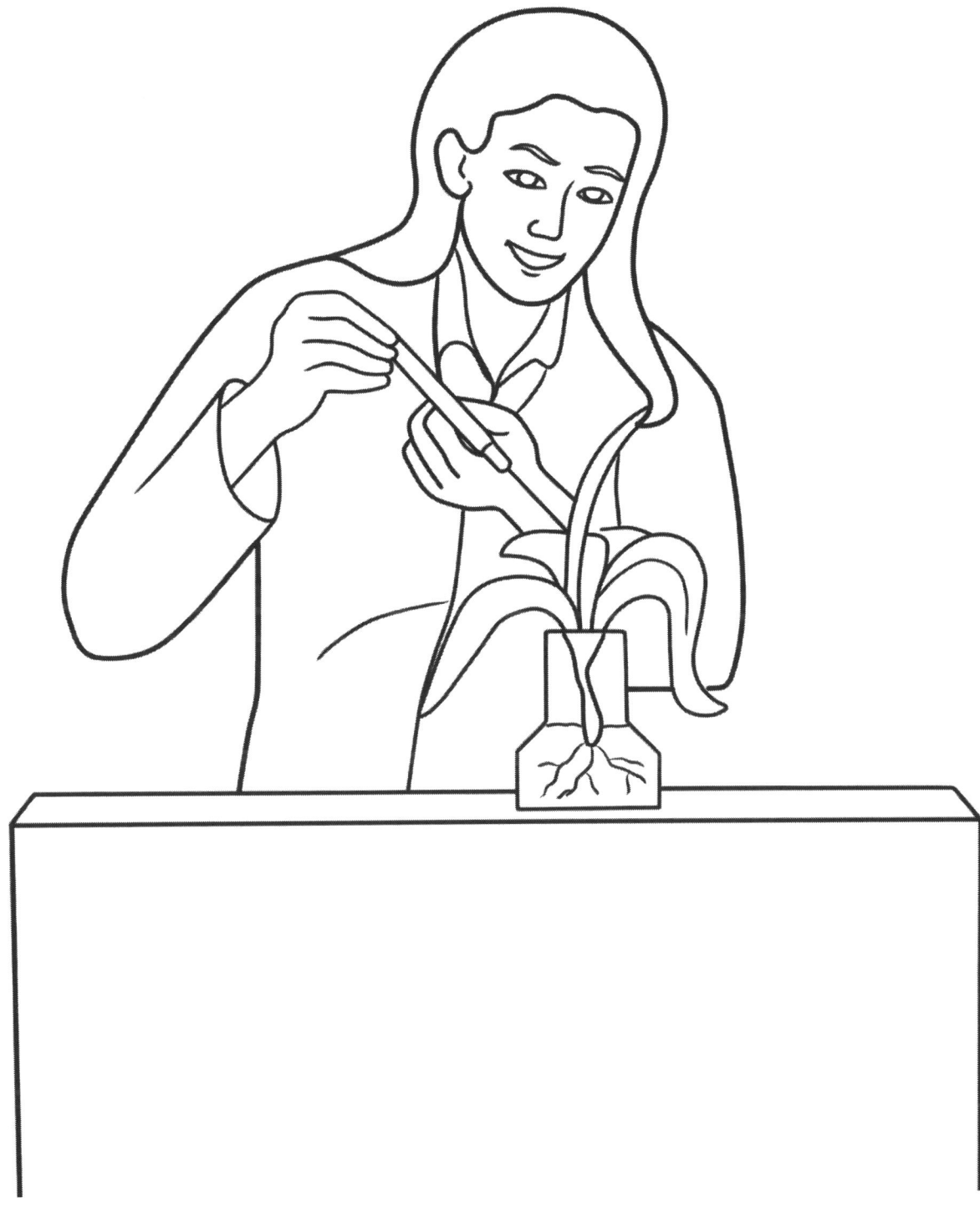

Exploring STEM Occupations Activity Book

Urban Planners

Develop plans for land use in urban areas. $42,200/yr. $66,900/yr. $99,600/yr.   6 yrs. college   Small occupation.

Slower than average growth.   Moderate number of annual openings.   Level of interest 1 2 3 4 5

Public Health Educators

Carry out health education programs. Educate people about healthier lifestyles and where help is available. $29,600/yr. $50,400/yr. $90,300/yr. 4+ yrs. college Small occupation. Faster than average growth. Few annual openings.

Level of interest 1 2 3 4 5

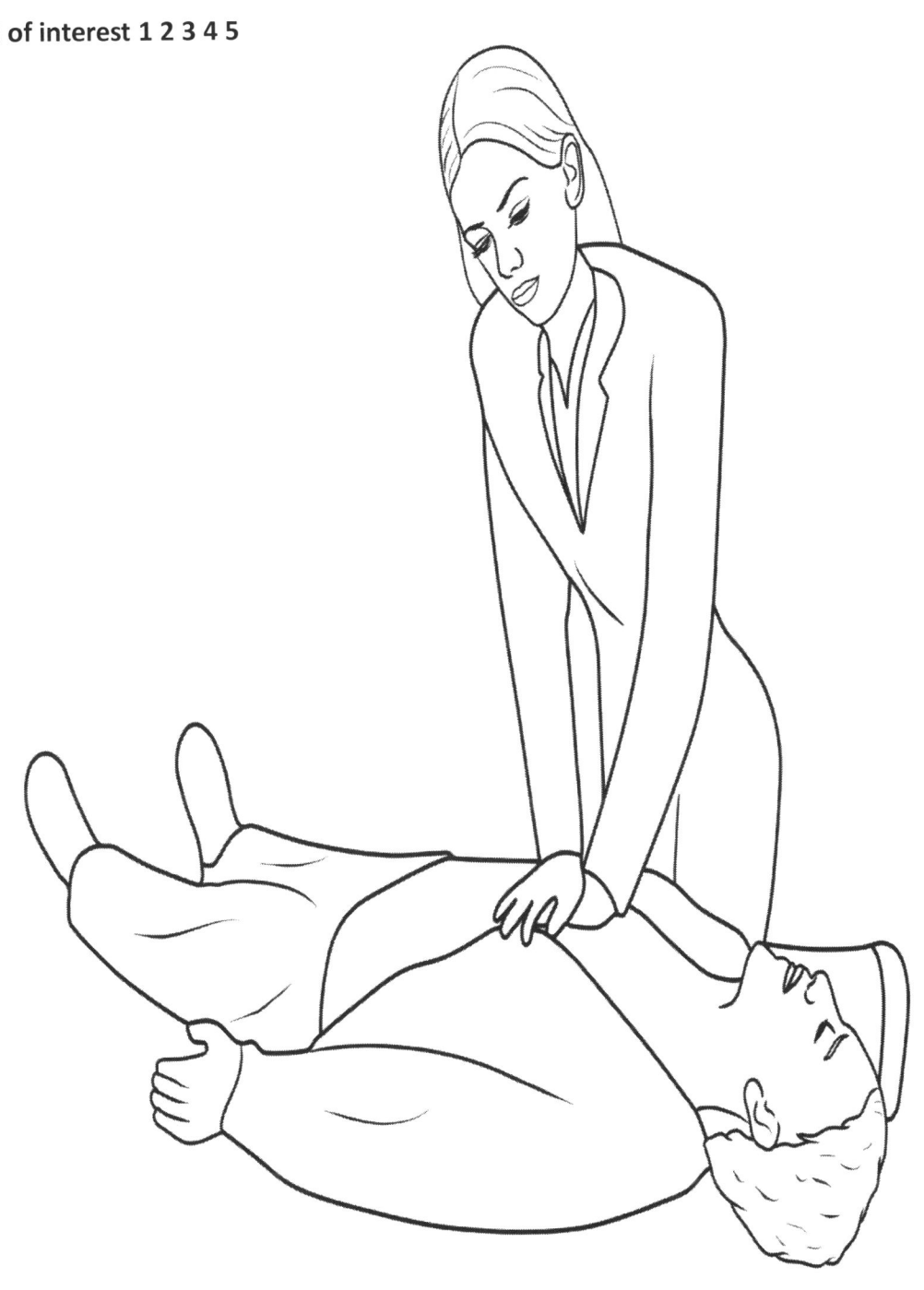

Exploring STEM Occupations Activity Book

Orthodontists

Diagnose problems with patient's teeth & fit braces to correct problems. Must be able to get along with people, be precise as mistakes can cause injury to patients, and like to help people. $79,000/yr. $187,200/yr. $187,200++/yr. 9+ yrs. college Small occupation. Average growth. Moderate number of annual openings. Level of interest 1 2 3 4

They didn't hurt as much as my compound fracture!!

Pharmacists

Dispense drugs prescribed by physicians and other health care providers. Must be exact when filling orders, able to explain possible side effects of prescription, and able to stand all day.

$89.300/yr. $121,000/yr. $150,600/yr.   9 yrs. college   Large occupation. Much faster than average growth.   Very high number of annual openings.

Level of interest 1 2 3 4 5

Exploring STEM Occupations Activity Book

Doctors

Help keep us healthy. Must be able to communicate with others: to teach, give advice, and help with medical problems. $187,200/yr.+ 9 yrs. college   Medium size occupation.   Average growth.   Moderate number of annual openings.   Level of interest 1 2 3 4 5

Why do doctors make more than teachers?

m gnihta ddA ?uoy rof htaw od yeht taht wollI

Physicians & Surgeons Specialties

Indicate your preferences. You might want to consider which types are on-call 24/7 & which have mostly regular office hours.

- ☐ Physicians & Surgeons – MD & DO
- ☐ Acupuncture
- ☐ Adolescent
- ☐ Allergy – Immunology
- ☐ Anesthesiology
- ☐ Arthritis
- ☐ Asthma
- ☐ Aviation
- ☐ Bone & Joint (Orthopedic)
- ☐ Cancer (Oncology)
- ☐ Cardiovascular
- ☐ Child Birth
- ☐ Chiropractic (DC)
- ☐ Colon & Rectum
- ☐ Colon & Rectum Surgery
- ☐ Cosmetic Surgery
- ☐ Dermatology
- ☐ Dermatology Surgery
- ☐ Diabetes
- ☐ Digestive & Liver
- ☐ Ear, Nose & Throat
- ☐ Emergency Medicine
- ☐ Eye
- ☐ Eye – Pediatrics
- ☐ Eye Surgery
- ☐ Family Practice
- ☐ Foot & Ankle
- ☐ General Practice
- ☐ Glands (Endocrinology)
- ☐ Gynecology
- ☐ Gynecology Surgery
- ☐ Hand Surgery
- ☐ Head & Neck Surgery
- ☐ Heart (Cardiology)
- ☐ Infectious Diseases
- ☐ Infertility
- ☐ Internal Medicine
- ☐ Kidney (Nephrology)
- ☐ Lung (Pulmonary)
- ☐ Manipulative Medicine
- ☐ Naturopathic (ND)
- ☐ Neurology Surgery
- ☐ Neurology (Nervous System)
- ☐ Newborn – Infants
- ☐ Obesity Severe Surgery
- ☐ Obstetrics (Pregnancy & Delivery)
- ☐ Occupational Medicine
- ☐ Oncology
- ☐ Opthalmology (Eye)
- ☐ Optometrists
- ☐ Orthopedic (Bone & Joint)
- ☐ Orthopedic Surgery
- ☐ Otology (Ear)
- ☐ Pain Control
- ☐ Pathology
- ☐ Pediatrics (Infant, Child, Adolescents)
- ☐ Pediatrics Surgery
- ☐ Physical Medicine & Rehabilitation
- ☐ Plastic & Reconstructive Surgery
- ☐ Podiatric (D.P.M.)
- ☐ Podiatric Surgery
- ☐ Pregnancy
- ☐ Preventive Medicine
- ☐ Proctology
- ☐ Psychiatry, Child
- ☐ Psychiatry, General
- ☐ Pulmonary
- ☐ Radiology
- ☐ Radiology, Therapeutic
- ☐ Rheumatoid & Arthritic Conditions
- ☐ Rhinology (Nose)
- ☐ Skin
- ☐ Sleep Disorders
- ☐ Spine Surgery
- ☐ Sports Care
- ☐ Urgent Care
- ☐ Urology
- ☐ Urology Surgery
- ☐ Vascular (Blood Vessels)
- ☐ Weight Control
- ☐ Wound Care
- ☐ X-Ray

Exploring STEM Occupations Activity Book

Radiologists

Are doctors who interpret x-rays and other medical images. They also administer radiation treatments. Must be able to communicate with others. They like to teach, give advice, and help with medical problems.

$56,600 /yr. $187,200+/yr.   Additional info. NA   9 yrs. college   Medium size occupation. Fast growth.   High number of annual openings.   Level of interest 1 2 3 4 5

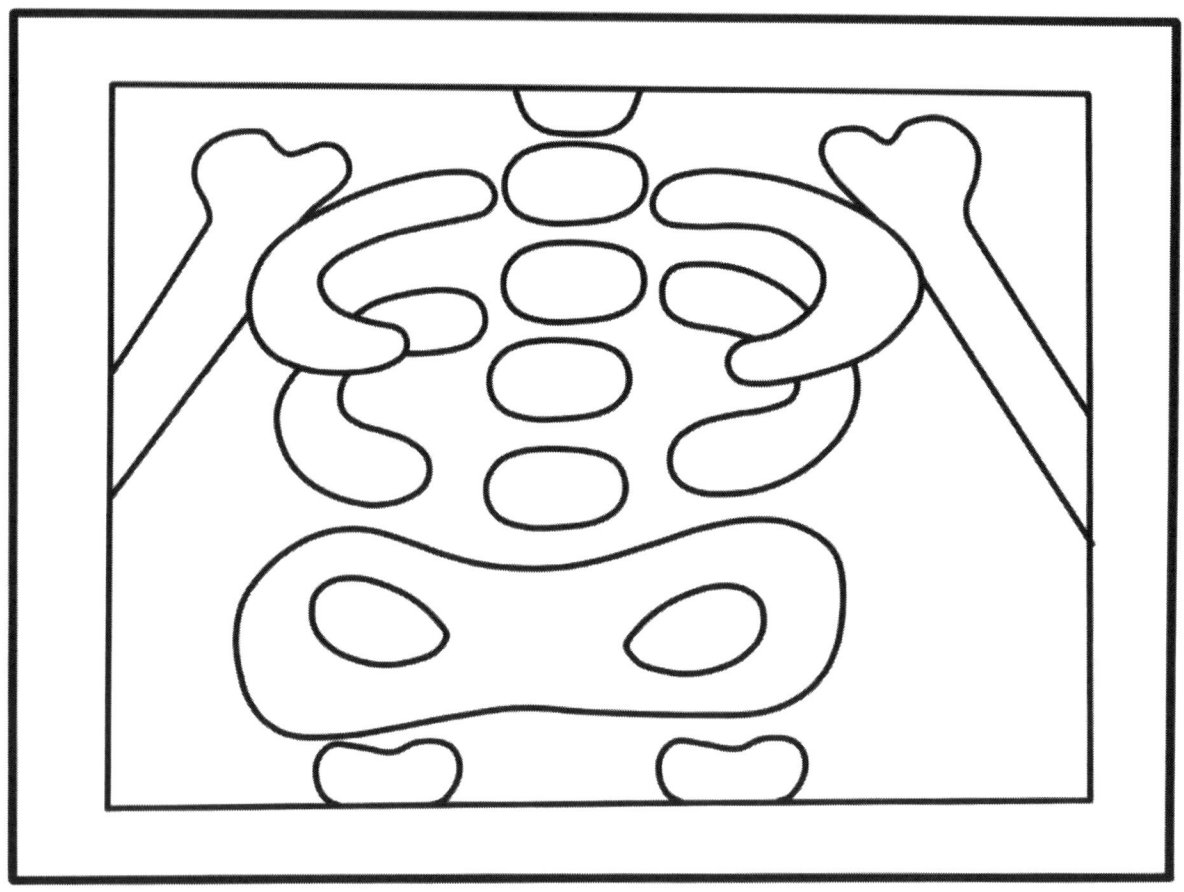

Exploring STEM Occupations Activity Book

Radiologic Technologists

Use special equipment to create images of internal organs, tissues, and bones. Constantly talk to doctors and patients. $37,600/yr. $55,900/yr. $80,100/yr.   2 yrs. college   Large occupation.   Faster than average growth.   High number of annual openings.   Level of interest 1 2 3 4 5

Radiation Therapists

Give radiation treatments to patients to treat cancer. Like being independent & make decisions on their own. $53,500/yr. $80,090/yr. $118,200/yr.   2 – 4 yrs. college   Additional Information N.A.   Level of interest 1 2 3 4 5

Medical Sonographers

Listen to taped recordings of medical procedures and transcribe them into written reports. Use medical dictionaries to insure proper terminology is used. $46,900/yr. $34,750/yr. $93,800/yr.   High School +   Medium size occupation.   Slower than average growth.   Moderate number of annual openings.   Level of interest 1 2 3 4 5

The following are occupations that have similar work duties, skills, be in the same career ladder, or have similar education.   They may be in a different level of pay.

❑ Nuclear Medicine Technologist

❑ MRI Technologist

❑ Dental Hygienist

Level of interest 1 2 3 4 5

Exploring STEM Occupations Activity Book

Physical Therapists

Help patients improve or correct their physical disability. They also recommend preventative healthcare exercises. $55,800/yr. $82,400/yr. $116,100/yr.   4 – 6 yrs. college   Medium size occupation.   Much faster than average growth.   Moderate number of annual openings.   Level of interest 1 2 3 4 5

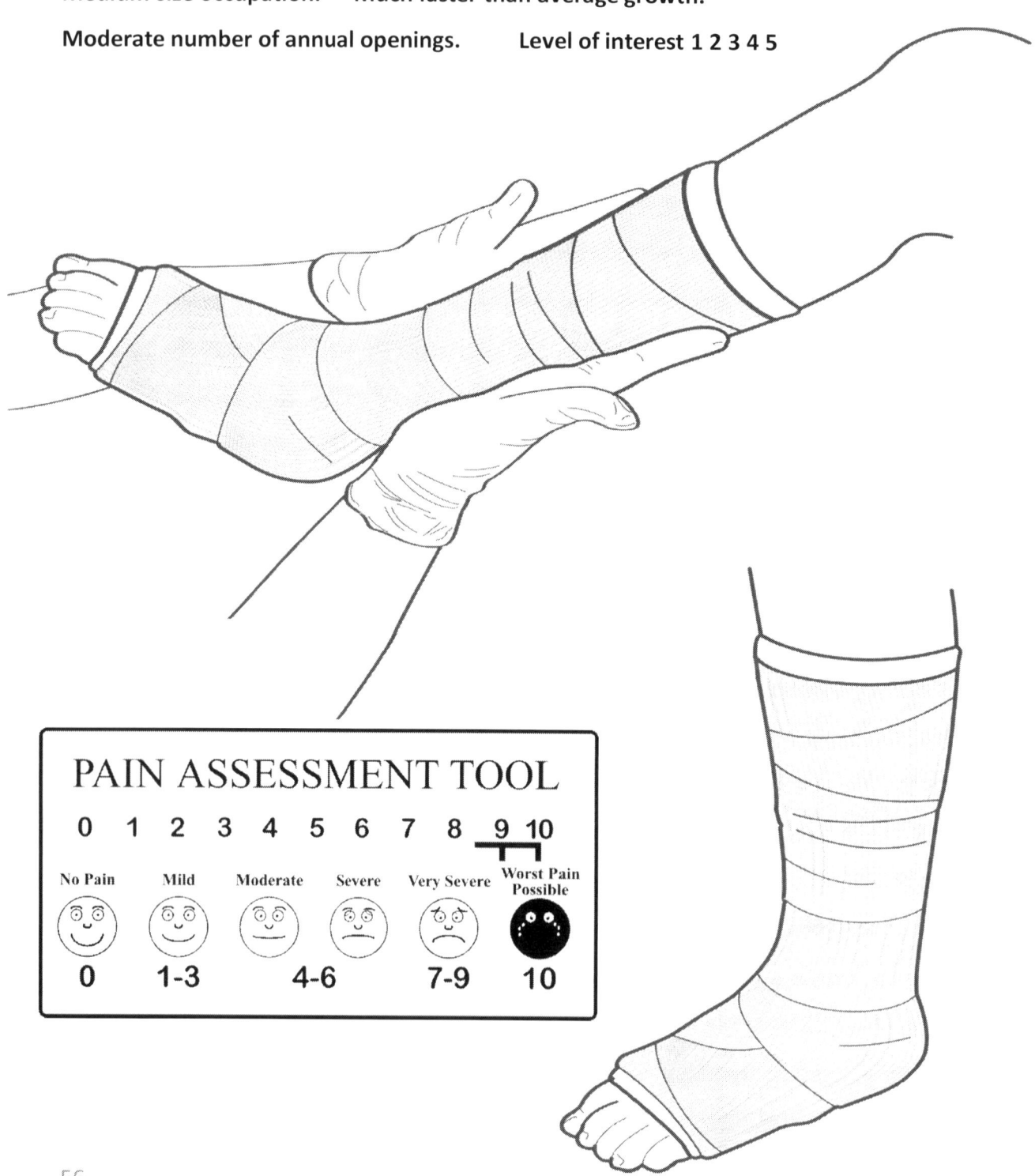

Exploring STEM Occupations Activity Book

Computer Science STEM Occupations

Using websites from computer companies & the military, add additional occupations. Indicate your level of interest 1 2 3 4 5. Complete chart for occupations rated 3+. Use pencil. Today's Date _____.

Occupation / Job Description	Education	Income	Level of Interest
Computer Hardware Engineer			1 2 3 4 5
Cryptologic Linguist			1 2 3 4 5
Computer User Support Specialist			1 2 3 4 5
Computer & Information Scientist			1 2 3 4 5
Military Intelligence			1 2 3 4 5
Computer Science Teacher			1 2 3 4 5
Patriot Launching System Enhanced Operator			1 2 3 4 5
Computer Detection Systems Repairer			1 2 3 4 5
Computer Sales Person – Business			1 2 3 4 5
Computer Science Sales Person - Consumer			1 2 3 4 5
Geospatial Intelligence Imagery Analyst			1 2 3 4 5
Computer Numerically Controlled Programmers			1 2 3 4 5

Exploring STEM Occupations Activity Book

Computer Technicians

Install and maintain computer systems. Must be able to talk with users to determine needs and problems.

$28,300/yr. $$47,600/yr. $80,200/yr.   High School + 2   Medium size occupation.

Slower than average growth.   Moderate number of annual openings.

Level of interest 1 2 3 4 5

Career Clusters Interest Inventory

Check the activities that interest you in each box. Add each column. Total your answers to discover which career clusters you may want to explore.

- ❏ Taking care of pets in your neighborhood
- ❏ Working in a garden and creating landscapes
- ❏ Planting and taking care of flowers and plants
- ❏ Transplanting small trees
- ❏ Nursing sick animals back to health
- ❏ Brushing or grooming dogs, cats, and/or horses
- ❏ Hiking thought forests and watching wildlife
- ❏ Chopping wood and replanting trees
- ❏ Identifying environmental hazards and sick/dying plants

Total checks _____

- ❏ Performing with the school's drama club
- ❏ Performing (music, drama, dance) for an audience
- ❏ Using a computer to create graphic designs
- ❏ Creating an original video or film
- ❏ Sketching or painting pictures
- ❏ Taking photographs
- ❏ Writing poems, stories, and plays
- ❏ Working with jewelry, sculpture, ceramics or stained glass
- ❏ Designing a newspaper layout (artwork)
- ❏ Being a disc jockey for an amateur radio station

Total checks _____

- ❏ Using a cash register
- ❏ Typing minutes of a school club meeting
- ❏ Filing or sorting mail or other papers
- ❏ Running your own business
- ❏ Designing a website
- ❏ Managing tasks for a group
- ❏ Preparing reports and analyzing data
- ❏ Typing documents for other people
- ❏ Volunteering to answer phones

Total checks _____

- ❏ Repairing small appliances
- ❏ Using tools to make household repairs
- ❏ Cutting and shaping wood to build structures
- ❏ Volunteering to work for Habitat for Humanity
- ❏ Drawing house or building floor plans
- ❏ Building simple circuit boards
- ❏ Working as a sound &/or lighting technician
- ❏ Laying brick or cinder block
- ❏ Painting houses or buildings
- ❏ Landscaping and planting flower gardens

Total checks _____

Exploring STEM Occupations Activity Book

Career Clusters Interest Inventory

Health Science

- Taking care of a sick relative
- Watching doctor/hospital shows on TV
- Learning first aid and CPR
- Volunteering at a local retirement home
- Volunteering as a hospital aid
- Using a stethoscope to listen to someone's heart
- Identifying human body parts from a diagram
- Bandaging sports injuries with a trainer's help
- Assisting persons in wheelchairs in daily tasks

Total checks _____

Hospitality & Tourism

- Working in a restaurant
- Planning vacations and other functions
- Cooking, baking, and serving meals
- Participating in sports or recreational activities
- Being a lifeguard
- Catering a function
- Working in a concession stand
- Exercising and working out
- Officiating a sporting event

Total checks _____

Finance

- Planning a mock stock market game
- Investing money and studying investments
- Balancing a checkbook
- Opening a savings/checking account
- Being a treasurer for a school club
- Organizing a fund-raiser
- Collecting money for a school or community event
- Developing a budget
- Using spreadsheets and financial computer programs as an income tax volunteer

Total checks _____

Education & Training

- Working as a kids' camp counselor or volunteer
- Tutoring young children
- Reading to elementary school students
- Giving instructions for/or directing a play on stage
- Baby-sitting young children
- Organizing and shelving library books
- Peer counseling or mediation
- Helping special needs children
- Teaching young children in an after school program

Total checks _____

Exploring STEM Occupations Activity Book

 # Career Clusters Interest Inventory

- ❏ Listening and helping friends with problems
- ❏ Serving food at a homeless shelter
- ❏ Working with the elderly
- ❏ Shopping, comparing prices, & consumer goods
- ❏ Volunteering to be a Big Brother/ Big Sister
- ❏ Making a family menu
- ❏ Participating in youth groups or community organizations
- ❏ Working as a dietetic aid
- ❏ Delivering food and clothes to people during the holidays
- ❏ Volunteering at a local retirement home

Total checks _____

- ❏ Reading mystery novels and trying to solve clues
- ❏ Playing "Clue" or other mystery board games
- ❏ Watching mystery movies or "courtroom dramas"
- ❏ Listening to a police scanner
- ❏ Running errands/volunteering for a lawyer's office
- ❏ Following court cases in the news
- ❏ Participating in training to be an EMT
- ❏ Volunteering to search for missing pets or persons
- ❏ Participating in search and/or rescue training

Total checks _____

- ❏ Flying airplanes
- ❏ Repairing vehicles, bikes, and engines
- ❏ Working in a warehouse or taking inventory
- ❏ Operating motorized machines or equipment
- ❏ Visiting space camps
- ❏ Building and repairing boats
- ❏ Operating a CB or ham radio
- ❏ Reading mechanical and automotive magazines

Total checks _____

- ❏ Developing software programs
- ❏ Building computers
- ❏ Playing video games and interactive games
- ❏ Surfing the Internet
- ❏ Learning how to configure operating systems
- ❏ Installing software
- ❏ Learning how to assemble computer hardware
- ❏ Playing with electronic gadgets
- ❏ Designing video games

Total checks _____

Exploring STEM Occupations Activity Book

Career Clusters Interest Inventory

- ☐ Campaigning for a political candidate
- ☐ Making political speeches
- ☐ Volunteering as an urban planning committee member
- ☐ Running for class office
- ☐ Planning and preparing budgets
- ☐ Participating in a debate
- ☐ Volunteering as a legislative aide
- ☐ Learning and speaking a foreign language
- ☐ Researching and writing grants

Total checks _____

- ☐ Cutting and styling hair
- ☐ Selling products for a school fund-raiser
- ☐ Taking tours of new houses for sale
- ☐ Designing or modeling clothes
- ☐ Giving people advice on products they should buy
- ☐ Decorating your house and rearranging furniture
- ☐ Hosting a yard sale
- ☐ Arranging and selling flowers
- ☐ Fixing watches and clocks

Total checks _____

- ☐ Visiting science museums
- ☐ Building model aircrafts, boats, and trains
- ☐ Exploring caves and collecting rocks
- ☐ Watching the weather and tracking storms
- ☐ Stargazing
- ☐ Using a computer to solve math riddles and equations
- ☐ Identifying plants, animals, and/or marine life
- ☐ Developing solutions to environmental problems
- ☐ Designing experiments
- ☐ Learning about different cultures

Total checks _____

- ☐ Welding or working with metals
- ☐ Repairing and upholstering furniture
- ☐ Creating wood carvings
- ☐ Taking machine shop classes
- ☐ Making belts or other leather goods
- ☐ Operating a printing press
- ☐ Installing and repairing home stereo equipment
- ☐ Sewing, weaving, knitting, or other needlework
- ☐ Building cabinets, shelves, and other simple wood working

Total checks _____

Exploring STEM Occupations Activity Book

Totals

Count the check marks in each section and place the total in the following boxes. Each group is a career cluster. Career clusters are groups of similar occupations. These clusters are a way to narrow down the hundreds of career options to a general area of interest.

My top 3 interest areas:

_____   _____   _____

| 1
Agriculture, Food, & Natural Resources
_____ | 2
Arts, A/V Technology & Communications
_____ | 3
Business, Management & Administration
_____ | 4
Architecture & Construction
_____ |

| 5
Health Sciences
_____ | 6
Hospitality & Tourism
_____ | 7
Finance
_____ | 8
Education and Training
_____ |

| 9
Human Services
_____ | 10
Law, Public Safety, Corrections & Security
_____ | 11
Transportation, Distribution & Logistics
_____ | 12
Information Technology
_____ |

| 13
Government & Public Administration
_____ | 14
Marketing, Sales & Service
_____ | 15
Science, Technology, Engineering & Mathematics
_____ | 16
Manufacturing
_____ |

Exploring STEM Occupations Activity Book

Draw a picture of yourself at your first choice career choice today.

Plan B _____.

Additional books available:

Exploring STEM Occupations – Grades K-2

Exploring Bright Outlook Occupations – Grades 4-6

Exploring Education & Training – Grades 7-10

For more information:

careeractivities@gmail.com

Made in the USA
San Bernardino, CA
13 October 2015